Eyes and Ears
Work Hard

Brenda Ferry

MACMILLAN

First published 1993
Reprinted 1995

Published by MACMILLAN EDUCATION LTD
London and Basingstoke
*Associated companies and representatives in Accra, Banjul,
Cairo, Dar es Salaam, Delhi, Freetown, Gaborone, Harare,
Hong Kong, Johannesburg, Kampala, Lagos, Lahore, Lusaka,
Mexico City, Nairobi, São Paulo, Tokyo*

ISBN 0-333-58143-1

Printed in Hong Kong

A catalogue record for this book is available from the
British Library.

Series editor: Lorna Evans

Illustrations by George Craig

Chapter
| 1 |

It was nearly Christmas and everyone was on holiday. Obi was thinking about all the things that happen at Christmas. It was a lovely time, the best time of the year.

Ike was in his room doing his holiday homework. He liked finding out about things and writing everything down. Sometimes he forgot to do his homework because he was so busy writing about other things!

Obi walked into his room. "Ike, you're not still writing, are you?" she asked.

"Of course I am," replied Ike. "I've got lots to do. I've got lots of interesting books and newspapers to read too."

Obi was quiet for a moment. Then she asked, "Well, what are you writing about?"

Obi wanted to visit her cousins, Chinwe and Emeka. Ike wanted to visit them, too, but he wanted to finish his work first.

"I'm writing about the cotton plant and how cloth is made. There are lots of different . . ."

Ike couldn't finish explaining because, just then, Mother called up the stairs.

"Obi! Obi, where are you? Chinwe's here and asking to see you. I'm just going to market. If you both want to come with me, you'd better hurry up!"

"Oh, good! Yes please and hello!" Obi answered. She ran down the stairs to greet her cousin. Chinwe laughed because Obi often tried to do everything at once. Obi was very funny and made everyone laugh a lot. Chinwe was her best friend as well as her cousin.

"Why are you going to market?" asked Chinwe.

"I need palm oil, but I want to look at some cloth too. We all need new dresses for Christmas," Mother replied.

Obi and Chinwe liked going to market. There were always so many people buying and selling different things. The market was noisy, hot and dusty, but there were lots of things to see.

They went to the place where cloth was sold first of all. Because everyone wanted new clothes at Christmas, there were many different sorts of cloth to look at and buy.

"Can we buy this beautiful blue one?" asked Chinwe. Blue was her favourite colour.

"Come and look at this one!" called Obi. "It's red and has white stars on it. Mother, where are you? Come and see what we've found."

Mother was standing by a stall in the middle of the market. She was looking for Trader Tim. She always bought cloth from him. She was a very good customer. Trader Tim had promised to bring her some new cloth with special Christmas patterns.

But Trader Tim was not there. In his place was a new trader nobody knew. This trader had the most beautiful cloth Mother had ever seen.

"Obi! Chinwe! Come and see this!" she called.

The girls ran along the narrow path between the stalls to see what Mother had found.

"Oh, oh, oh!" said Obi, and her eyes grew very large indeed. Chinwe didn't say anything. She just opened her mouth and looked in surprise. Then she very gently lifted her hand and touched the cloth with one finger. It really was very, very beautiful.

The new trader said, "Now look hard at this. This cloth is called lace. I found it especially for this market. I don't have much of it, as you can see, but I know you people here like good cloth."

The lace was pink and shiny and had hundreds of tiny holes in the pattern. Small pieces of thin cloth, cut into the shape of flowers, were sewn all over it. In the middle of each flower was a small, shiny stone. It was lovely.

Mother said, "That's true. We do like good cloth and this is good lace. I'll buy some, just a little, if you give me a good price."

Mother and the new trader talked for some time and then

3

decided on a high, but fair, price. At last the new trader took Mother's money and picked up his scissors to cut the lace.

Then something terrible happened. Instead of cutting the lace, the trader picked it all up, put it under his arm and ran away. Nobody saw where he went.

"Stop! Stop! Stop thief!" cried Mother loudly, at the top of her voice.

Obi and Chinwe couldn't believe what they saw. For a second they stood quite still. Then, as soon as they heard Mother's cries, they tried to follow the new trader through the crowd. Mother tried to chase him too. All the people in the market wanted to catch him as well.

Everyone looked for him everywhere. They looked under tables, behind sheds, in the road and on the railway line. People talked, shouted, threw their arms about and looked all over the place. But the trader had just disappeared.

Chinwe asked all the market people who were nearby, "Do you know that new trader, the lace man? Does he have any friends here?"

None of them knew his name because they hadn't seen him before. None of them could say a good word for him, either, because he'd been rude and unfriendly to them.

"We don't want to see that lace trader in the market ever again. He's a bad man and nobody wants him as a friend," everyone said.

Chapter
| **2** |

Mother was crying because she had lost her money and because the thief had got away. Now she had no money to buy palm oil either. It was terrible and they were all very upset.

Chinwe was thinking hard about the lace trader and trying to remember exactly what he looked like. She said to Obi very quietly, "You know, we must tell Ike and Emeka about this as soon as we get home."

Obi nodded her head. "I agree," she replied, and nodded her head again.

Both Chinwe and Obi were thinking the same thing. There was only one way to find that horrible trader, the lace man, and that was for Eyes and Ears to start working again.

Eyes and Ears was a secret. Everybody knew that Obi and Ike and their cousins Chinwe and Emeka were friends but nobody knew about Eyes and Ears. They called themselves this name because they liked finding out about things. They liked solving difficult problems. They used their eyes to see things and ears to hear things.

"Shall we go home?" asked Obi. She was feeling very sad because her mother was so unhappy. Mother didn't want to go at first, but she agreed in the end.

"Well I don't think we'll find that new trader here now," she said. "You're right. We may as well walk home."

They walked home slowly, talking together, trying to remember everything. At last, Obi said, "You know, I think that new trader was frightened by someone. That's why he ran away."

Mother and Chinwe stopped to look at Obi. Obi was good at guessing and sometimes she was right.

Mother listened to her. "Well, it's true that lots of people

5

wanted the lace. He could have sold all of it if he hadn't run away," she agreed.

Chinwe was frowning. "I know who frightened the new trader," she said at last. "It was a policeman." She turned to Obi. "He came along the path from the vegetable market just as your mother took her money out of her bag. I saw him myself. That policeman frightened the trader."

They walked home along the railway line because that was the quickest way to go. Neither Mother, nor Chinwe, nor Obi spoke again because they were all feeling so miserable.

When they arrived at the house Ike and Emeka were watching football on television. Ike was curled up in a big chair. He didn't greet them or take his eyes off the television, so he didn't see they were upset.

"Emeka's come to see the football," he said. "Nigeria is playing against Kenya in the Africa Cup! It's very nearly finished."

Ike still did not look up from the television. Usually he did not like football very much but this game was important and exciting.

Emeka was not sitting down. He was jumping up and down and, at the same time, watching the game very carefully. His eyes were shining and he was shouting at the television.

"Come on, come on, come on, Oti! Play the ball!" he cried.

There was no point in speaking to either Ike or Emeka until the game had finished. Mother, Obi and Chinwe went into the kitchen. They would have to wait a few minutes before they could talk to the boys.

"I wish Father was here. He'd know what to do," said Obi. "When is he coming home?"

"Today or tomorrow," replied Mother, "but the harmattan is blowing. He's stuck in Lagos."

The harmattan blew from the north every year in December. It carried fine red dust into the air. Often the pilots couldn't see and the aeroplanes couldn't land.

At that moment, Emeka and Ike rushed into the kitchen and asked for a drink. They were thirsty after watching the game.

"We won!" shouted Emeka.

"They were playing in Nairobi and . . . Mother, what's the matter?" asked Ike.

Mother was not smiling as she usually did and there was no drink on the kitchen table for them.

"Mother's lost some money and we saw the person who took it. That's what's the matter," said Obi.

"The money was stolen when we were in the market and we couldn't catch the thief," added Chinwe.

"It all happened so quickly and it surprised me. I'm upset and angry at myself as well as angry with the thief," said Mother.

There was so much to explain, but neither Obi nor Chinwe nor Mother knew where to start the story.

They all needed a drink badly. Obi found some Fanta in the store and put some groundnuts on the table.

"We didn't buy anything in the market in the end," said Mother and she started to cry again. "We didn't even get the palm oil for cooking our food."

"We'll all try to help you now," said Obi slowly, making big eyes at Ike and Emeka and looking hard at them. She was trying to tell them there was work for Eyes and Ears.

Chapter

| **3** |

Neither Emeka nor Ike understood exactly what was the matter because they hadn't been told. However, Ike knew that Obi was trying to say something to them, and Emeka knew that they needed palm oil. To Emeka that was most important.

"I'll go and get palm oil from our house if you like," he said.

"I'll come as well," Ike added. "Emeka, wait while I pick up my notebook. Mother, you can tell us about the thief when we come back."

"That's a good idea," said Mother. She didn't want to tell her story in a big hurry and Emeka was always in a hurry if he was hungry.

Emeka left the house, crossed the railway line and started to run up the narrow path. He always hurried everywhere. Ike followed behind as fast as he could. Suddenly Emeka stopped. He stopped because he heard a very loud bang. Then he heard some shouts and people crying and talking very loudly.

Emeka turned round. "What was that? Did you hear that, Ike?" he asked.

"Yes, what was it?" Ike replied.

They both stood still. Ike listened for a moment before adding, "Wait a minute while I write it in my book. There may be work for Eyes and Ears."

"Let's go and see what's happened first," said Emeka. "You can write it all down later. The noise came from the road."

Although he was hungry, Emeka had forgotten the palm oil.

The two boys ran on together. When they reached the

corner at the end of the path, they stopped and looked down the main road.

"Look at that!" shouted Emeka. "An accident! That's what made the noise. That mammy wagon has fallen on its side!"

The mammy wagon was about a hundred metres away, but Ike and Emeka could see everything. People were climbing from it, calling out loud to each other and looking for their loads. Other people were running to help.

Suddenly Emeka gripped Ike's arm.

"Look," he shouted. "Over there, by the mammy wagon. Look at that man. What is he doing?"

"Which man?" asked Ike. "Who do you mean? There are lots of men."

"The fat man in the green shirt," Emeka answered angrily. "He's pushing everybody about. He's not helping at all."

It was true. As Emeka was speaking the fat man roughly pulled a little boy to his feet. The child had hurt his leg in the accident, and was resting on a sack. The man took no notice

of him. He just picked up the sack and threw it over his shoulder. Then he picked up more loads and ran off as fast as he could.

"I'm going after him," Emeka cried. "He's up to something. Nobody does that sort of thing at an accident."

Emeka set off, but even though he was a good runner, it was difficult to catch up with the fat man. The mammy wagon was blocking the road, and there were cars and bicycles and lorries everywhere. Crowds of people were trying to see the accident, and help if they could. Chickens and goats had escaped and were chasing round in circles, followed by their owners. And yams and tomatoes and suitcases full of clothes and all the other loads lay in the road.

Ike ran after Emeka, but he kept bumping into people and all the traffic got in his way. It was no good. He knew he would never catch up.

Ike decided to write everything down in his notebook

11

instead. He wrote down the time and the date and the place where the accident happened. He described the mammy wagon and took its number. He even copied the words on the front of the mammy wagon – NO CONDITION IS PERMANENT. He did not understand what this meant, but perhaps it was important.

Then he drew a map which showed where the mammy wagon had crashed and how the loads had fallen. It took a long time, but he wanted to get it right.

After that Ike looked round for the driver. The man was sitting by the side of the road with his back to the accident. He did not help anybody, or ask for help to mend the mammy wagon. Nor did he seem to be worried! Ike thought that this was very strange, so he wrote it down too.

Ike decided to speak to the driver so he went up to him. Then another strange thing happened. The driver started to laugh!

"One big accident," Ike heard him say. "That's what they got. One big accident."

"Are you talking to me?" Ike asked.

It was the driver's turn to be surprised.

"Go away!" he shouted, turning to Ike and jumping up angrily. He stamped his foot and waved his arms. "This is nothing to do with you. Mind your own business. Go away."

Ike was not going to give up so easily. Something was going on, and he wanted to know what it was.

"What happened?" he asked. "Why did you have the accident?"

"Why does anybody have an accident?" the driver shouted. "The tyre blew out, of course. Can't you see? The tyre blew out and over we went."

The driver stopped. Then he pushed his face next to Ike's and breathed, "There were nails in the road. Can you hear? Nails in the road. That was the problem."

"He's mad," thought Ike. "First he's laughing, then he's trying to frighten me. What's this all about?"

"Nails," the driver breathed again. "Don't you under-stand? Nails. That was the problem."

Chapter

| **4** |

It was not until late that afternoon that Eyes and Ears could talk.

Mother was waiting for Ike and Emeka when they arrived home, and she was not pleased with them. "Where have you been?" she asked. "Where's the palm oil?"

In all the excitement Ike and Emeka had forgotten about it. This made Mother even more cross.

"Go and get it *now*," she told them. "And don't stop for anything on the way. I need it today, not next week."

By the time they had fetched the palm oil and helped Mother to cook and eaten the food and washed the dishes afterwards, the day had almost gone.

"Right," said Ike when at last Eyes and Ears were alone. "Chinwe, put the television on so nobody will hear us. We've got a lot to tell you. I have written it all down."

Chinwe put the television on, but before Ike could start his story, she closed his notebook.

"No," she said. "It's our turn first. Obi and I have waited all day to tell you about the thief in the market. It's work for Eyes and Ears, and just as important as your story."

Ike did not really like this. But Obi and Emeka agreed with Chinwe, so he had to agree too.

"Oh very well," he said. "Get on with it."

Obi told the boys about the lovely lace in the market.

"It was pink and shiny and it had little flowers sewn all over it," she said. "And in the middle of each flower there was a tiny stone. It was the most beautiful cloth you ever saw."

Ike was thinking.

"I know about cloth," he said. "It's my holiday home-work. We make lots of cloth here in Nigeria."

"Yes, but not like this lace," cried Obi.

"I'm not so sure," Ike went on.

Emeka sighed loudly. He knew what was coming next. Ike was going to tell them all about cloth. They would all have to listen – and Emeka did not like listening.

"We grow cotton in the north," Ike went on. "Machines make the cotton into cloth. Sometimes it's thin and fine, for making clothes. Sometimes it's thick, for making blankets. It's very good cloth, and it's sent all over Nigeria in lorries."

"Some of it's sent by aeroplane," Chinwe broke in. "It's cheaper to send small loads that way. Trader Tim brings his cloth in by aeroplane, and a lorry collects it from the air-port."

"How do you know that?" asked Ike.

"Somebody in the market told me this morning," Chinwe replied. "The aeroplanes can't fly at the moment because of the harmattan, so Trader Tim's cloth didn't arrive. That's why he wasn't there today."

Ike nodded his head.

"Interesting," he said. "I didn't know that."

"What about the thief?" asked Emeka. He did not find cloth at all interesting. He wanted to hear the best part of the story, about the thief.

So then Chinwe told them about the new trader, and how he had run away with Mother's money.

"And he just disappeared," Chinwe ended her story. "Nobody knew who he was, or saw where he went."

Ike wrote everything down in his notebook.

"What did the new trader look like?" he asked. "Can you describe him?"

"He was quite small and dark," said Obi. "And young."

"Can't you think of anything else?" asked Ike. "There are millions of small dark young men."

Obi shook her head, but Chinwe suddenly remembered, "There was something else! It was his hands."

"What about his hands?" asked Ike. "Everybody has hands."

"These hands were different," Chinwe said. "They were horrible. They were a funny shape, and they had white marks on them. That's why I remember them. Such beautiful cloth in such horrible hands."

Ike described the thief in his notebook and Eyes and Ears talked about him for a few more minutes. But nobody had anything else to add. And nobody knew how to get Mother's money back.

"OK," said Chinwe at last. "Now you can tell us about the accident."

Ike sat up in his chair and turned the pages of his note-book. This was the time that he loved.

First he told Chinwe and Obi all about the mammy wagon, its size and its colour.

15

"It had NO CONDITION IS PERMANENT written on the front," he explained. "I shall know it if I see it again."

Next he told them about the accident, how the lorry had fallen on its side, and how the passengers and their loads had fallen out.

Then he told them about the driver, how he had laughed and then got angry.

"I don't understand about the nails," he finished. "I want to look in the road myself."

All this time Emeka was getting more and more jumpy. He could never sit still for five minutes, but this was worse than usual.

"You've forgotten all about the most interesting thing," he burst out at last. "What about the fat man? You haven't talked about him at all. You've forgotten him."

For a second Ike's face fell. He had forgotten about the fat man. And in the hurry to get home, he had not written anything about him in his notebook.

"You tell us then," he said to Emeka. "You saw him. You chased him."

So Emeka told the others about the fat man.

"He was pushing people around," he said. "That's why I noticed him. He wasn't helping at all. When he found his loads he just picked them up and ran off with them as fast as he could. He didn't care about anything else. He just wanted to get away."

"What did he take?" asked Chinwe.

"Three or four big sacks," Emeka replied. "I don't know what was in them."

"Where did he go to?" asked Obi.

"I'm not sure. I couldn't catch him. There were so many people around. I followed him as far as Chief Agu's house, and then he just disappeared."

"Chief Agu's in America at the moment," Ike said. "I read about him in the newspaper."

"Well perhaps he didn't go into Chief Agu's compound," Emeka cried, "but that's the last place I saw him."

Ike wrote everything down in his book.

"There's a lot to think about," he said. "But we've got to do something now, before it's too dark."

Chapter

| **5** |

"Mother, we're just going out. We may go to Auntie's house," Obi called over her shoulder as Eyes and Ears left their own compound.

She wanted Mother to know where they were. But as it was getting dark, Mother might stop them. Eyes and Ears had to get away quickly.

They did not wait for Mother's answer. They hurried over the railway line and along the back path to the main road.

"What do you want to do?" Emeka asked Ike when they were well away from home. Emeka liked doing things, not just talking.

"I want to look at the place where the mammy wagon crashed, and I want to look for nails on the road," Ike answered. "The driver said that nails made the tyre blow out, but I don't believe him."

All the passengers and their loads had gone, and the traffic was moving along the main road again.

"There's the mammy wagon," Emeka whispered. "NO CONDITION IS PERMANENT, just as Ike said. I can see the driver too. We'll have to be very quiet."

The mammy wagon was still on its side and the driver lay next to it. He was not moving.

"He's fast asleep," said Ike. "Good. Now we can hunt for these nails."

Eyes and Ears crept along the road. They had to be really quiet. There were cars and lorries going up and down, but footsteps made a different noise. The driver might wake up at any minute and see them.

"Shhhhh . . ." Ike hissed as Emeka tripped over a stone.

Emeka frowned at him.

"I can't help it," he replied. "My feet are too big."

Eyes and Ears reached the mammy wagon, and still the driver slept. Ike pointed to the front of the mammy wagon. Obi would look there for nails. Emeka would look behind it. He and Chinwe would work near to the driver because they were the quietest.

Eyes and Ears hardly dared to breathe but they got on with their work. Once Chinwe knelt down and touched the ground. The others were sure that she had found something.

"No, no" she whispered, shaking her head. "I made a mistake."

After five minutes Ike pointed to the back path. Eyes and Ears understood at once. It was time to leave. Nobody had found anything, and the driver might wake up at any moment.

A few metres from the mammy wagon Emeka stopped. He stared down at the road, very interested in something. Then at last he followed the others along the road.

It was almost dark as Eyes and Ears crept through the shadows to the back path. Once they were off the main road everybody talked at once.

"I was so frightened . . ." Obi began.

"The driver nearly . . ." Chinwe broke in.

"I didn't see . . ." Ike tried to explain.

"Listen to me!" Emeka shouted so loudly that everybody stopped. "There weren't any nails by the mammy wagon. The driver told a lie. We all know that. But did you see the tyres?"

Nobody else had looked at the tyres. They were all too busy looking for nails.

"Tell us, Emeka," Chinwe said. "What about the tyres?"

"They were worn out," Emeka explained. "And worse than that, there was no air in two of them."

"No air," breathed Ike. "That's dangerous."

"Very dangerous," agreed Emeka. "With tyres like that anybody could have an accident."

Ike was thinking.

"Wait a minute," he said. "The tyres were dangerous, but that doesn't mean anything. Lots of people drive cars with worn tyres. That may not be important."

"It is important," said Emeka. "It's very important. I know because I saw something else on the road."

"What?" asked Ike. "There weren't any nails, I'm sure of that."

"Not nails," Emeka laughed. "Marks. Marks on the road."

Nobody understood him.

"What do you mean?" Obi asked. "What marks?"

"When a driver puts his brakes on hard the car stops

19

quickly and the tyres leave marks on the road," explained Emeka. "That's what happened. The driver put his brakes on hard. The marks on the road show that. Then the mammy wagon stopped quickly and fell over as it did so."

Ike was beginning to understand.

"You mean . . ." he began. "You mean that the driver wanted to have an accident. He knew what would happen. If he braked too hard, and his tyres were worn, he would crash."

"That's right," said Emeka. "He knew he would crash. He knew exactly what would happen."

Ike was still thinking.

"That fits in with the driver's words," he said. "I wrote them in my notebook. See, here they are. 'One big accident. That's what they wanted.' That's what the driver said after the accident."

Nobody spoke for a moment. Then Chinwe said, "So the driver made the accident happen. But who wanted it? That's the question now. Who told the driver to crash? And why?"

"I can only think of one person," said Ike. "The fat man. The man who Emeka chased. Mammy wagons don't usually stop on the main road. Perhaps he wanted to get off the mammy wagon. Perhaps he told the driver to crash. But it all seems very strange to me."

Obi gripped his hand.

"I've just thought of something," she said. She put her head on one side. She always did this when she had a good idea. "We've met two bad men today. First there was the new trader who stole Mother's money. Then there was the fat man at the accident. I think the two men know each other."

Chinwe stared at her.

"How can you say that?" she asked. "They were nowhere near each other. One was in the market and the other was here."

"I don't understand really," Obi tried to explain. "I just think they do. There aren't many bad people in this town, so I'm sure they all know each other."

"Let's think about it later,' said Chinwe. "It's time to go home."

Chapter
| **6** |

The sky was brighter the next day. The harmattan was not so thick and aeroplanes could land. Obi and Ike's father came home and everybody was very glad to see him.

Mother made egusi soup. Father liked egusi soup better than any other food. Somehow Emeka and Chinwe arrived just as it was ready!

Father told them about waiting for the aeroplane in Lagos. It seemed very exciting to Eyes and Ears.

"It wasn't exciting at all," said Father. "It was awful. Everybody wanted to travel on the same aeroplane. Everybody wanted food and drink. Everybody got angry and shouted at the woman in the ticket office. And it was very hot and very noisy."

"Did you eat at the airport?" asked Mother.

"Eat at the airport?" cried Father. "There was nothing to eat or drink. I'm very happy to be home. Now what's happened while I've been away?"

Eyes and Ears looked at each other. They wanted to keep their secrets, at least for a little while.

"Are you going to tell Father about the new trader?" Obi whispered to Mother.

"What's that? What are you saying?" cried Father.

Obi sighed. There was only one problem with her father. He heard everything, even if you did not want him to.

"What's happened?" Father asked again. "Tell me."

"Well it's not very important," Mother began. "We went to the market yesterday to buy cloth. We found a new trader who had the most beautiful lace. But just as I was paying him he ran away with my money and the cloth."

"Oh no," said Father. "Did you try to catch him? Did you tell the police?"

"He disappeared, and nobody knew him," Mother explained. "I did tell a policeman, but they won't catch him now."

"It was such lovely cloth too," added Obi.

Father frowned and put down his spoon. Eyes and Ears knew that he was worried.

"Do you know that smugglers are bringing cloth into Nigeria from other countries?" he asked.

Everybody stared at him. Nobody knew about smugglers.

"Why do they do that?" asked Ike at last. "We make our own cloth in the north. I read about it for my homework."

Ike liked to understand everything, and he always had lots of questions.

"Smugglers don't pay taxes," Father explained. "So they are stealing from the whole country. And because they don't pay taxes they can sell their cloth at a better price than people like Trader Tim. They hurt people like him too."

"That's terrible," said Chinwe. "He's such a nice man. He always tries to find good cloth for his customers."

"It is terrible," Father went on. "And it's bad for the people who grow cotton and the people who make the cloth too. They can't sell their cloth these days."

Nobody was enjoying the egusi soup very much now. Eyes and Ears were listening hard, and Mother was nearly crying. She was remembering her lost money.

"Do you think the new trader was a smuggler?" Mother asked. "He nearly sold me some beautiful lace."

"I'm sure he was," Father said. "The smugglers bring lace and very good cloth into Nigeria. They know we like the best things here."

Now Mother really was crying. Obi held her hand. She hated to see her mother so sad.

"Don't cry," said Father. "I'm sorry that you lost your money. But it's better to lose your money than buy from smugglers."

"We've got to find them," Ike said softly. "We've got to stop those smugglers."

"*No*," said Father. He had heard every word. "You mustn't do anything. You children must keep out of trouble. This is work for the police."

"But Father . . ." cried Ike.

"*No,*" said Father, even more firmly. "These smugglers are dangerous. Just keep out of trouble."

Nobody said anything else. They did not have to. They all agreed about one thing though. This was work for Eyes and Ears.

The problem was that nobody knew what to do.

Eyes and Ears were sitting outside, talking about the smugglers. Ike had written everything down in his notebook, but even that did not help.

"It's no good," he said at last. "I've thought and thought about the smugglers, and I'm not getting anywhere."

"Too much thinking's not good for you," said Emeka. "I found that out a long time ago."

"Don't be so foolish," Ike said. "You do say some silly things sometimes, Emeka."

Emeka jumped to his feet angrily.

"Oh please sit down, Emeka," cried Obi. She hated quarrels. "Ike didn't mean anything."

"I only said . . ." Ike began, but Emeka was really angry now.

"I'm not going to listen any more," he shouted. "I've listened for too long. I'm going to do something instead."

Everybody stared at him. Emeka did not often get angry, but when he did, things happened.

"You're all talking about the smuggler. What about the other problem? What about the accident? What about the fat man?"

"What about him?"

"I'm going to find him, that's what," shouted Emeka. "That's what I'm going to do. I know where I saw him. Near Chief Agu's compound. I'm going to look for him."

"But you can't just go there," cried Chinwe.

"Please wait a bit," begged Obi.

But Emeka would not listen.

"Just watch me," he cried.

And with that he ran off towards the chief's house.

Chapter

| **7** |

For a moment nobody said a word. This was serious!

Firstly none of them had ever visited Chief Agu's house. The chief was an important man, and children did not do that sort of thing.

And secondly, it could be dangerous. Emeka had seen the fat man near the chief's compound. Nobody knew who the fat man was, but they did know that there was something strange about him.

Obi was nearly crying.

"What shall we do?" she whispered in a small voice. "We've got to do something. Emeka may get into trouble. He may need our help."

"We'll think of something." Chinwe tried to smile, but she too was worried about Emeka. After all, he was her brother.

Ike frowned. He was thinking hard.

"We'll give him fifteen minutes," he said at last. "If he's not home then we'll go and look for him."

Chinwe did not say anything else. She just got up and fetched the clock from the kitchen.

Ike, Chinwe and Obi sat and watched the clock. The minutes had never passed so slowly. The hand seemed to take forever to move.

When a quarter of an hour had passed there was still no sign of Emeka.

"Right," said Ike. "Let's go."

The three children hurried along the main road to Chief Agu's house. They noticed that the mammy wagon had gone, but there was no time to talk about that. They stopped at the gate of the chief's compound and looked in.

"Something's wrong," cried Obi. "I can feel it. Something's wrong."

There was something wrong with the house. It was locked up. All the doors and windows were closed, even though it was daytime. And there was nobody about. Where was Emeka? What was happening?

"Shall I go and look for him?" asked Obi. "I know Chief Agu's servant. I sometimes buy eggs from him. I could ask Nelson."

"Ask Nelson what?" said a voice right behind them.

Eyes and Ears could not believe their ears! Nelson was speaking. Where had he come from? Why had they not seen him before?

The servant laughed.

"Don't look so worried. I just got off the bus," he explained. "You were so interested in the house that you didn't see me."

"Have you been away?" Ike asked. He was thinking very quickly. "Is Chief Agu's house empty?"

Now it was Nelson's turn to be worried.

"I had a message three days ago," he told Eyes and Ears. "A friend told me that my father was sick. A man asked him to tell me. He said that I should go to my village at once I went, but when I got home my father was not sick at all. It was a mistake."

This was another strange thing for Eyes and Ears to think about.

Ike was still thinking.

"Shall I carry your box?" he asked, pointing to the large box by Nelson's feet.

If he carried Nelson's box, he would be able to go into Chief Agu's compound without any nasty questions. And he had to go in. Emeka might be there, and in trouble.

Nelson was surprised because people did not often help him.

"Thank you," he said, and opened the gates wide.

Ike picked up the box and he and Nelson went up the drive to the house. Obi and Chinwe followed quickly behind.

They went past the garage to the back of the house. They waited near Nelson's quarters. Nobody was there either, and everything was very quiet. Where was Emeka?

Suddenly Nelson stopped.

"Look! *Chai*! Look!" he shouted loudly.

"What's the matter?" asked Ike.

Chinwe and Obi felt a little frightened as they went to see what was wrong.

"The door to my quarters! It's open. I'm sure I locked it before I went away. What's happened?"

Nelson ran to his quarters and quickly came out again.

"Someone's been here," he cried, tears running down his face. "What am I to do? Have thieves gone into Chief Agu's house as well?"

Nelson was so worried, he did not know what to do. He did not know whether to cry, shout or see if anything was missing. He was very frightened. He had promised not to leave the house while Chief Agu was away.

It was horrible. Ike, Chinwe and Obi wanted to find Emeka. Nelson wanted to find the person who had been in his quarters. Would Nelson think Emeka was a thief? Where was Emeka? Where was the fat man? Nobody knew what was happening.

There was no time for Ike to write anything in his notebook. There was no time to draw maps of the chief's house. They would have to remember all they saw.

Then something else happened.

Obi heard the sound first of all. "I think I can hear a car," she said, and ran to the corner of the house.

"Quick, quick," she called a moment later. "Somebody's opened the garage doors. There's a car inside."

Nelson said, "There can't be. Chief Agu took the car to Lagos."

Obi called again, "Come! Come quickly! Be quick!"

Chinwe and Ike ran to the corner of the house just in time for the three of them to see a big black car in the garage. Before anybody could stop it the car came out of the garage, along the drive, and out through the open gate.

Chapter
| **8** |

The only thing Ike, Chinwe and Obi could do was look in the garage. The doors were wide open but there was nothing there at all except a small, closed door at the back.

"Where does that little door go to?" Ike asked Nelson.

"It doesn't go anywhere. It's a storeroom," Nelson replied.

Chinwe tried the handle of the door. "It's locked," she said.

"It can't be locked. It's never locked." Nelson replied.

"Oh, but it is. Come and see," said Chinwe.

Nelson was not really interested in the door at all but he did go to see.

"Dear me!" he said. "What am I seeing! I need new eyes! I don't believe what I see, but you're right. Look at this padlock. I can't open the door."

"Where's the key?" asked Ike.

He did not know what else to say. They had to find Emeka. They could not leave the chief's compound until he was found. Where on earth could he be?

"How do I know where the key is? I never saw this padlock before," Nelson said angrily. He wasn't interested in this problem. He had to find out if anything was missing from Chief Agu's house.

Nelson soon left Eyes and Ears to look in the garage for themselves. This was just what they wanted.

Ike, Chinwe and Obi stood and looked at the door. They all felt it was important but they didn't know why. Then Obi put her head on one side as she always did when she had an idea.

"Listen! I think I know where Emeka is," she said.

"I don't believe you. How can you know?" asked Chinwe.

"Where do you think he is then?" asked Ike.

"Well," said Obi slowly, "We can't see him anywhere. So he must be in that storeroom. He must be there because he's nowhere else."

"But we can't hear him," said Chinwe. "Emeka always makes a noise. He can't be there."

"He is there," said Obi again, very firmly. Obi was often right when she had an idea. Ike listened to her because she might be right this time too.

"There must be some way of looking into that storeroom," said Chinwe. "Let's go to the back of the garage and look."

Ike led the way. They had to walk over a yam patch to get to the back. It made their shoes very dirty. But when they looked up, they saw a small window, high up in the garage wall. It was open.

"That's lucky," said Ike.

"We need a chair to reach up and look inside," added Chinwe.

"I'll go! I saw one earlier!" Obi said and rushed off. She had seen a chair near Nelson's quarters. It was hard work carrying it back.

Ike put the chair into place and all three climbed on to it. The problem was that the chair was not really high enough. They had to stand on their toes to see through the window. The storeroom was very dark and it was difficult to see at first.

"There's nothing there," said Ike.

"There must be," said Obi.

"Wait a minute," cried Chinwe. "Shut your eyes for a few seconds, Ike, and then look. You'll be able to see better. It's always difficult to see in the dark when you've just been in the sun. Look in the corner. I'm sure there's something there."

"There is," Obi agreed, "and it's moving about."

"It's a sack," said Chinwe.

"It's a sack of yams," cried Ike.

"Don't be foolish," said Chinwe crossly. "Nobody puts yams in sacks. And yams don't move."

"It's Emeka!" shouted Obi.

All three just stared at the moving sack. It was difficult to

believe, but it was true. Emeka must be in the sack. But how could they get him out when the window was so high? They would have to get help.

"I'll go and get Nelson," said Ike. "He's bigger than we are. He can climb into the storeroom and get Emeka out."

Nelson thought Ike was playing and didn't believe him at first.

"You imagine too much, you children," he said. "I look for this thief and you find a magic sack! No, no. Go home now."

"Please, Nelson! Please come. I helped you carry your box," said Ike.

At last Nelson agreed to go with Ike.

"All right! All right," replied Nelson unhappily. "I'll climb in and look for you and then you must go home."

Obi and Chinwe were waiting by the window for them. Nelson said nothing at all. Chinwe, Ike and Obi watched as he climbed into the storeroom. They stood on the chair to see what he was doing.

"*Chai!*" they heard him shout. "What is this?"

"It's Emeka!" shouted Chinwe, Ike and Obi from the window.

Nelson sat back on his heels. He did not know what to think.

"Come on, Nelson," said Chinwe. "There's no time to sit down now. Cut that rope, the rope round the sack. Let Emeka out."

There was nothing to say. Nelson cut the rope and seconds later he and Emeka were both standing in the yam patch.

Ike said, "Thank you, Nelson. You're one of our best friends. You've helped us a lot. We'll help you when you need it too."

Nelson smiled. He didn't know that his new friends were Eyes and Ears and they really would help him.

Chapter

| **9** |

As soon as they were back home by themselves, there were questions.

"Are you all right? What happened?"

"How did you get into that sack?"

"Why didn't you call out?"

"I'm all right," replied Emeka.

He felt tired and thirsty. His clothes were dusty. He had stones in his shoes. He just felt miserable and didn't want to talk at all.

"We must know what happened," said Ike, taking out his notebook. "Tell us everything."

"There isn't much to say," explained Emeka. "I went round to the back of Chief Agu's house. The door of Nelson's quarters was open, so I knocked. Somebody came out. He looked at me, but didn't say anything for a time. Then he asked me what I wanted."

"What did you say?" asked Chinwe.

"I asked him when Chief Agu was coming back," replied Emeka. "Then he got really angry. He asked me why I was there and what I knew. He asked lots of questions, but he didn't listen to me."

"Who was he?" asked Ike. "Was he the fat man?"

"No," Emeka replied. "He was small and thin."

"What happened next?" asked Chinwe.

"It was very strange. He didn't give me time to speak."

"But what happened?" asked Chinwe again. She thought Emeka told his story very slowly.

"Wait a minute," said Emeka. "It's difficult to say. I must remember everything. The man didn't look at me as he spoke. He looked past me."

"Was he looking at something behind you?" asked Ike.

"I don't know," Emeka replied. "I was looking at his hands. They were horrible. All white and ugly."

"Go on," said Ike.

"Well suddenly somebody put something over my mouth. I don't know who he was."

"He must have come up behind you," said Chinwe. "Perhaps he was the fat man."

"It could have been. I couldn't see," said Emeka, "and I couldn't shout either. He tied something over my face. Then he put a sack over my head. He tied me up and carried me away. He had big, strong arms. I didn't know where I was or anything. I couldn't escape. The next thing I knew, Nelson was cutting me free."

"Oh how horrible," Obi cried. "You were so brave, Emeka. Are you OK? Did they hurt you?"

"I'm fine," said Emeka. "I'm tired though. There was no air in the sack and I couldn't breathe."

Everybody sat quietly for a moment. They were all thinking the same thing. Emeka could have been hurt, or even killed. What if the men had left him tied up in the storeroom? What if nobody had found him or he had never escaped?

It was all too horrible. Chinwe got up and fetched some groundnuts and soft drinks from the kitchen. That would make Emeka feel better.

Ike stopped writing in his notebook and sucked his pencil. Then he frowned. The others knew Ike was thinking hard.

"It all fits into place," he said at last. "I understand now. Well I understand some things."

"I don't understand anything," said Emeka. "And I'm the one who did all the dangerous work."

Ike, Chinwe and Obi did not agree with this at all, but nobody said a word. After all, Emeka had had a terrible time.

"You'd better explain," Emeka sighed. He didn't want to talk any more, but he was too tired to say so.

Ike took a deep breath.

"First of all, the thin man," he began. "He had horrible white hands. Emeka saw them. But Chinwe saw somebody with horrible white hands too. The new trader. The smuggler who stole Mother's money."

"You're right," cried Chinwe. Her thoughts were racing ahead. "It must be the same person. There can't be two people with hands like that in one town."

Obi and Emeka agreed and waited for Ike to go on.

"Secondly, the fat man," he began. "We don't know so much about him."

"I know a lot about him," Emeka broke in. "I know he ran away from the accident. I know he tied me up in a sack. I felt his big arms."

Ike shook his head.

"But we don't know that it was the same person," he said firmly. "We think it was, but we're not sure. Just as we think he's a friend of the man with the white hands. We think he is, but we're not sure."

"I'm sure." Ike always wanted to avoid making mistakes, but Emeka was not going to be put off.

"I'm sure he wanted the accident to happen, too," he went on. "He wanted the driver to crash the mammy wagon. And I'm sure he's a smuggler."

"I think you're right," Ike agreed at last. "But here's an interesting question. Why did he want the mammy wagon to crash?"

Emeka stared at him.

"So he could get off, of course," he said. "So he could get to Chief Agu's house quickly. He didn't want anyone to see him near the market with so many loads. He wanted to hide the loads in a safe place. He didn't want to get caught."

Ike was listening hard. He had not thought about this, but he knew that Emeka was right.

"I've got something to say." Obi could not keep quiet any longer. "I know why Chief Agu's house was a safe place. Because he wasn't there. The house was empty. And the smugglers knew that. They read about it in the newspaper, just as you did, Ike."

"You're right, Obi!" cried Chinwe. "I've just thought of something else. The message that Nelson had. Do you remember?"

"What message?" asked Emeka.

"You didn't hear about it," Chinwe went on. "Nelson got a message. Somebody told him that his father was sick, so he went back to his village. But it wasn't true. His father was fine. Nelson thought it was all a mistake, but it wasn't. Somebody gave Nelson that message so he would leave Chief Agu's compound. Somebody wanted the whole place to be empty."

"Wait a minute," said Ike. "Let me think."

"Don't you see, Ike? The two of them are smugglers. They knew that Chief Agu was away, and they made sure that Nelson left too. They wanted to use the compound for a few days, just while they sold the smuggled cloth."

Chinwe was so excited that she was shouting.

"Wait a minute," Ike said again. "I've got to write this down."

Chapter

| **10** |

The next day there was a birthday party. Eyes and Ears had been working so hard that they had forgotten about it. But when they remembered they were happy. After all, everybody likes parties.

"Emeka, go and clean your shoes," his mother said. "How did you make them so dirty? But hurry up. You'll be late."

Emeka rushed off to clean his shoes. He lifted the first one up and put his hand inside.

"What's this?" he thought.

He looked, and then looked again. Then, very carefully, he picked something up.

Just at that moment Mother called, "Emeka, come on. We're going."

There was no time to do anything. Emeka hurried after his mother and Chinwe. But in his pocket he had a secret.

All the children at the party looked very nice. The girls wore pretty dresses and the boys wore white shirts and trousers. The birthday cake was pink and blue and had eleven candles on it. It stood on a large, round table.

There was another table full of food. There was Fanta, lemon and Coca-cola to drink. There was rice, chicken, meat, ice-cream, coconut sweets and chocolate cake to eat as well. It looked beautiful. Everybody looked at the food and everybody was hungry.

Afterwards Emeka wanted to play football but nobody else was interested. Ike went to play a party game. He had to cut out words from newspapers and make up new sentences. He then had to run to be the first with the answer. Emeka did not like that sort of game at all. He thought it was boring.

Instead of playing, Emeka looked at the pictures in the newspapers. Somehow they seemed important, though he

could not think why. He looked at that day's paper first of all because the latest news always seems best. He turned the pages until he came to the pictures of cars, engines, wheels and tyres. Emeka loved looking and learning about all these things.

Then he saw a photograph of a mammy wagon which had just been lifted after an accident. Its tyres were being changed by the roadside. He looked at it for quite a time before he saw the name on the front of the mammy wagon. It said NO CONDITION IS PERMANENT! Emeka sat quite still. Then he looked around to make sure no one was looking. And then he tore the photograph out of the paper and put it in his left pocket.

Emeka put the photograph in his left pocket because he already had a secret in his right pocket. Now he had a real problem. He had two secrets and he couldn't tell anyone while he was at the party. So he ran round and round the room as fast as he could with his arms out. He was trying to be an aeroplane.

All Emeka could think was, "I've got two secrets in my pockets and nobody here knows."

It really was too much to think about, so he just ran.

Luckily, the party finished soon after that and it was time to go home.

As soon as Eyes and Ears were by themselves Chinwe said, "What were you doing, Emeka, making so much noise? Everyone will be cross with all of us, not just you."

"It wasn't fair," said Obi. "We won't be asked to a party ever again."

The girls were cross with Emeka.

"You don't understand anything," Emeka answered back.

"What don't we understand? What is there to understand?" Chinwe really was very angry.

Ike spoke quickly. "Listen to what Emeka has to say. I don't know what it is but I know it's important. I saw him at the party and I think he found out something. What is it Emeka?"

Emeka was pleased Ike understood. He said, "Yes, Ike, I think I did. Well, I found out two things and two things are a lot of secrets, and I couldn't tell you then."

"Well?" asked Chinwe, Obi and Ike together.

"Well," said Emeka, putting his hand into his right pocket, "look at these." He held out two small shiny glass stones. "When I got home last night I thought I had stones in my shoes. I did. I found them just before the party. Here they are."

"They're beautiful. They must be a part of a necklace," said Chinwe.

Obi looked at them carefully. Then she said, "No, they're not. They have two small holes at the bottom so they're tiny buttons." She held the pretty buttons in her hand and kept looking at them.

"How could I have got buttons in my shoe?" asked Emeka.

That was a difficult question. Nobody could think of an answer. Then Chinwe said, very slowly, "Let's think. You must have got those stones in your shoe when you were trying to get out of that sack."

"But why were the stones in the sack?" asked Emeka.

Everybody thought hard, then suddenly Obi cried out, "Of course! I don't know why I didn't think of it before. I know where these buttons come from."

"What are you talking about Obi?" said Ike. "We've just said they must have come out of the sack."

"You don't understand at all," replied Obi. "They might have been in the sack but that's not what I mean. Look, Chinwe. That beautiful lace we saw in the market had the same shiny stones in the flowers. There was lace in that sack before Emeka was put in it!"

Eyes and Ears were all smiling.

"This proves we were right," Emeka said. "The fat man carried the lace in sacks. Those were his loads when he ran away from the mammy wagon. The two men are both smugglers."

"And they used Chief Agu's storeroom to hide the loads," added Ike. "We're getting somewhere at last."

Chapter

| **11** |

"Well, well, well," said Ike, writing again. "We know a lot of things, and we can guess a lot of other things. This is really good news."

Nobody was angry with Emeka any more.

"I've got something else to tell you," Emeka said. "Don't you remember? I had two secrets at the party. That's why I couldn't keep still."

Emeka was good at doing things, but he did not often find things out. He felt very proud of himself.

"Of course," cried Obi. "The first secret was so good that I'd forgotten the second one. Go on, Emeka. Tell us."

Obi was always glad when other people were happy. And she could see that Emeka was very happy.

Emeka pulled something out of his pocket.

"Here's my other secret," he said, putting a torn, dirty piece of newspaper on the table. Things that came out of Emeka's pockets were always dirty.

"What's this?" asked Ike.

"Well I was looking in the newspaper while you were playing the game," said Emeka. "I read the interesting parts."

Emeka did not mean the front pages, with the news, but everybody knew what he did mean. He was only interested in reading about cars and lorries – and sport, of course.

"You see," Emeka went on, "there's a new machine which can lift lorries that have crashed. This is a photograph of the machine lifting a mammy wagon."

"Well?" asked Chinwe. "Why is this interesting?"

"It's a new machine. The people who own it put the photograph in the newspaper. They want everybody to know about it."

"Well?" said Chinwe again. She did not think that this was very interesting at all.

"Look at the mammy wagon, and look at the people in the photograph. That's interesting."

Ike, Chinwe and Obi stared at the piece of newspaper.

"I can't see anything," said Ike, cleaning his glasses.

"That's because your eyes are no good," said Emeka. "Come on. You're not trying."

Chinwe smiled and picked up the piece of newspaper.

"I can see what Emeka's talking about now," she said, nodding her head. "I had to look hard though. It's the name on the front of the mammy wagon, isn't it, Emeka? NO CONDITION IS PERMANENT. This is the mammy wagon that crashed."

"Right," said Emeka. "Now can you see the driver? Here?"

Chinwe and Obi nodded.

"And this man next to him. Who's he?"

Emeka pointed to the photograph again. Ike still could not see anything very well, but Chinwe and Obi could.

"It's the new trader," shouted Obi.

"It's the smuggler," shouted Chinwe at the same time.

Emeka was so excited he jumped up and ran round the compound.

"That's what I thought," he said, sitting down at last. "And it's really important because this is the man who was in Nelson's quarters. And this man," he stopped and pointed at a third man in the photograph, "this man is the fat man."

Neither Ike, Chinwe nor Obi could say a word. It was not often that this happened to Eyes and Ears!

"This proves it," said Ike at last. "The three men know each other. They're all in it together."

Eyes and Ears were so excited that they all had to do something different for a few minutes. Ike started to write in his notebook, of course, and he had a lot to write about. Chinwe picked up a book and opened it. She did not read the book – her head was far too full for that – but she turned the pages. Emeka ran round and round the compound, jumping and skipping and hopping and shouting and making a lot of noise. Obi went to her room and took off her party dress.

Ten minutes later they were all sitting round the table again.

"So what are we going to do?" asked Emeka.

"Should we tell Mother and Father?" asked Obi.

"Should we tell the police?" asked Chinwe.

"Let's think," said Ike. This was what he always said. He was clever and he liked thinking.

"I don't want to tell anybody," said Emeka. "This is our secret. Eyes and Ears have worked really hard. Let's solve this problem ourselves."

"Those smugglers are dangerous," said Chinwe. "They've already tied Emeka up in a sack and left him in the storeroom. They could do anything. I'm frightened of them."

"We know a lot more about them than they know about us," said Obi. "That's good. We know who we're fighting against. They don't."

"Somebody's got to stop the smugglers," said Ike. "The question is, can Eyes and Ears stop them? And how?"

It was very difficult. Eyes and Ears really liked to do things alone. But could they catch the smugglers? Should they ask for help? Would anybody believe them? They didn't have very much to tell the police or their parents.

Obi was frowning and looking more and more worried.

"I've thought of something else," Chinwe said at last. "What about Chief Agu? Are we quite sure that he doesn't know about the smugglers?"

"Quite sure," said Ike. "He's a friend of Father's. He's a good man. And anyway, we know he's not even in Nigeria at the moment. He's in America with all his family."

"We've got to do something," Emeka said. "We can't let those smugglers escape. We've got to do something."

"If we're going to do anything, we've got to do it quickly," Chinwe said. "They won't stay here for long."

"It's too difficult," Obi shook her head. "We don't know their names or where they're staying now or anything."

"We do know where they work though," said Ike slowly, closing his eyes.

Everybody waited. When Ike spoke like that and closed his eyes he was thinking. This could be important.

"They work in the market," Ike went on. "That's where they sell their cloth."

Nobody moved, and nobody said anything.

"I know what we'll do," Ike opened his eyes at last and smiled. "Listen. This is our plan."

Chapter

| **12** |

Nobody slept very well that night. There was too much to think about.

Ike wrote in his notebook for a very long time. At ten o'clock his mother told him to switch his light off, but he had not finished. After that he used his torch. He hoped that his mother would not find out.

Emeka dreamed that he chased the smugglers and caught them and tied them up with strong rope. People thought that he was very brave. Emeka liked that a lot.

Chinwe dreamed that the smugglers chased her, and caught her and tied her up with strong rope! She did not like that at all!

Obi lay awake and worried. Would Ike's plan work? Would she do her work well? Would both those horrible smugglers escape? She was sure they were dangerous men.

Early in the morning they all met at Ike and Obi's house, but there was not much time to talk.

"Do you all understand the plan?" asked Ike. "Do you all know what to do?"

Chinwe, Emeka and Obi nodded.

"I hope it works," said Chinwe.

"We shall need some luck," said Ike. "But if we are lucky, everything will be fine."

"And if it isn't fine we can tell Mother and Father," Obi added. "You promised."

"Come on," said Emeka. "We're all ready. Let's get on with it."

Ike had to carry out his part of the plan alone. He thought that he should make a speech, like a soldier before a battle. The trouble was, he did not know what to say. In the end he just said, "Good luck. See you later."

"Good luck to you too," the others replied.

Ike set off along the main road into town. The road was always busy and full of cars and lorries and buses. There were lots of people walking too, and Ike joined the crowd.

He was wearing his old jeans and a very dirty pair of trainers. He wanted to look like everybody else. It was important that nobody noticed him.

As he passed the gate of his school he saw a group of his friends.

"Ike," they called. "Where are you going? Shall we come with you?"

"Not today, thanks," Ike answered and hurried on.

Outside the library he saw his teacher.

"Have you finished your homework?" she asked. "Are you coming to the library to study?"

"Not today, Miss," Ike said. "I've nearly finished it though. It won't take me long now."

Ike slowed down as he came near to the market. People took their time here. They met their friends and talked and laughed together. They searched for the best goods to buy. They argued over prices. They all enjoyed themselves.

Ike knew exactly what he had to do. He had to find the two smugglers, the fat man and the man with white hands. Then, when the fat man was alone, he had to give him a message.

Ike was the only one who could carry out this part of the plan. Emeka could not do it because both of the smugglers knew him. They had seen him at Chief Agu's house when they tied him up in the sack.

Chinwe and Obi could not do it because the new trader, the one with horrible hands, had seen them in the market already. They had been with Mother when he stole her money. He might remember them. And anyway, girls did not give messages to strangers.

Ike waited until the market was really busy and then started to search for the smugglers. If they were still in town he would find them quickly. After all, if they wanted to sell their cloth, they could not hide away. But they would not be with the other cloth traders. That was too dangerous even for the smugglers.

Ike was lucky and he was right. The smugglers were still in town, and they were not hiding. One was near the main gate and the other was near the lorry park. They each had just a few pieces of cloth that they could carry easily.

"Clever," Ike thought to himself. "They can both get away quickly if they have to."

Ike waited until the smuggler with the horrible hands had a good customer. A woman in a blue and gold wrapper and a big head tie was asking to see all his cloth. She looked very rich. She would keep him very busy.

Ike pushed his way through the crowd to the fat man.

"Please, sir, I've brought a message for you," he said, touching his arm.

"A message?" The man looked frightened. "Who from? Who gave you a message?"

"Please, he said he was your friend. He was a little man."

"A little man, you say."

"Yes, a little man. He had funny hands. He was by the main gate with somebody else," Ike explained.

The fat man looked happier when Ike said this.

"Well, what was the message?" he asked.

"Please," Ike said, "you must go to the storeroom at once and take all your cloth with you. Your friend will meet you there. He's found a very good customer."

"The storeroom," the fat man said, and started to pack up his loads. "Right. Go and tell him I'm on my way."

"Yes, sir," said Ike. "Please sir, can I help you?"

"Just do as you're told," the fat man said rudely. He did not thank Ike for the message or give him anything. "Now get out of my way."

Ike had told a lie, but he was not sorry. This man really was horrible, a smuggler and a thief. Ike hoped that the next part of his plan would work as well as this part.

He followed the fat man out of the market, through the lorry park, to a big black car. The man did not once look back. The first part of the plan had worked.

Chapter

| **13** |

Emeka, Chinwe and Obi waited for nearly half an hour after Ike had left. The waiting was very difficult. They all wanted to get on and do something.

"It's a good thing Mother's not here," said Obi. "If she was here we might have to help her."

"Where is she?" asked Chinwe. "She hasn't gone to the market, has she? She might see Ike there."

"She's gone to Nine-mile Corner to buy meat," Obi told her cousins. "I think we're all going to Omorka for Christmas. Mother hasn't said so, but that's what I think."

Chinwe and Emeka were very pleased. They would go to the village too, of course. They would all stay in the big house there with Grandfather. There would be singing and dancing, and they would meet all their friends. Christmas would be lovely.

Then they remembered Ike's plan. There was hard work for Eyes and Ears before they could go anywhere.

Chinwe looked at the clock which they had fetched from the kitchen.

"Five more minutes," she said. "Then it's time."

"Let's go now," said Emeka. "I can't wait one minute longer."

Chinwe and Obi knew that Emeka really meant it. He could never sit still and do nothing. If they did not move soon he might do something awful.

"All right," Chinwe agreed. "But you must walk to Chief Agu's house. You mustn't run. We don't want anybody to notice us today."

A little later they were kneeling down at the gate into the chief's compound. It was closed. The windows of the house were still shut tight and there was nobody around.

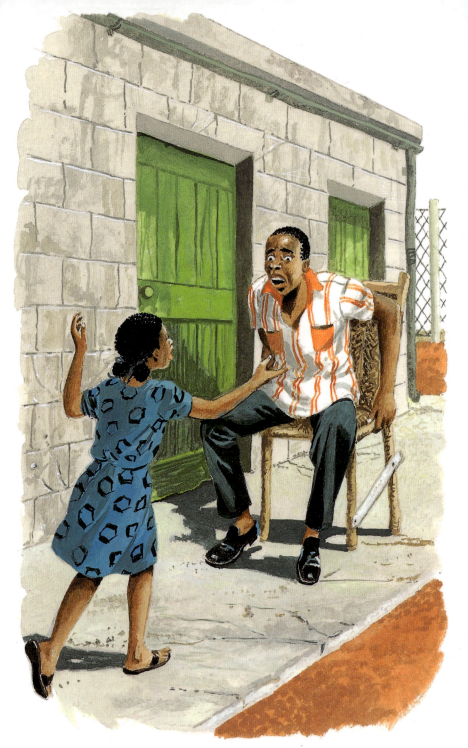

"Where's Nelson?" whispered Obi.

"I don't know," Chinwe answered, "but I'm sure he's somewhere near. He was so upset about leaving the house when he went to his village. He won't leave again. He'll be afraid that somebody else will break in."

"He's right to worry," Obi breathed, "because that's what we're going to do."

"Let's get on with the plan," said Emeka. "Obi, you know what to do, don't you? You've got to get Nelson out of the compound."

"I've got the worst job of all," Obi said. "I've got to play tricks on Nelson, and he's a friend. Why do I have to do this? It's not fair."

"You know why you have to do it," Chinwe said. "Because you are his friend. He'll believe you. He knows you better than the rest of us."

"Let's get the gate open and start work," said Emeka. "Now, are you ready Obi?"

Obi nodded.

"I'm going to close my eyes," she said. "Then I really shan't know who opened the gate."

It was not easy to open the gate and keep quiet at the same time. Obi heard feet on the drive and squeaks and heavy breathing, but she kept her eyes closed tight.

"We're in luck," said Emeka. "Nobody saw us. Now go on, Obi. Get Nelson out of the compound."

Obi tried to be brave as she walked up the drive. She took a quick look at the garage as she passed. That door was locked too, as she expected. That was work for Chinwe and Emeka.

At the back of Chief Agu's house she stopped. Her legs were shaking. Where was Nelson?

As she stood there Obi heard a noise, a very strange noise. It came from Nelson's quarters, but what was it? Was it Nelson? Was it a person at all? She knew that she would have to find out.

She crept towards Nelson's quarters. When she got there she nearly laughed out loud. The noise was coming from Nelson. He was fast asleep in a chair in the sun. The noise . . . Well if Obi was polite she would call it heavy breathing!

Suddenly Obi knew what she had to do.

"Nelson," she screamed. "Wake up. Wake up. Your chickens have escaped. The gate's open and they're running all over the road."

"What . . .? Where . . .? When . . .?"

Nelson leaped out of his chair. He did not know where he was. He did not know whether he was asleep or awake. He did not know who was speaking to him. He had no idea where his chickens were.

"Your chickens, Nelson," Obi screamed again. "They've escaped. Wake up! Your chickens have gone. They'll all be killed on the road. Quick! Quick! Follow me. I'll show you where they are."

Nelson did not even look in the compound to see whether Obi's story was true. He rushed along the drive after her, tripping over his own feet in his hurry. He was still only half awake. The only thing he knew was that his chickens were in danger.

"Look, the gate's open," Obi shouted.

"Who did that?" Nelson screamed. "Wait till I get my hands on him. Who left the gate open?"

Obi really could not answer that question. She was very glad that she had kept her eyes closed!

Chinwe and Emeka were standing at the gate.

"Stay here," Nelson shouted at them as he rushed past. "Watch the compound for me. Make sure that nobody comes in. Look after Chief Agu's house."

"Don't worry, we will," Emeka cried.

Obi did not give Nelson time to think clearly or decide what to do.

"Hurry, Nelson," she shouted. "Come on. The chickens were there, by the bus stop. I can't even see them now. Something must have scared them. Something made them run away. Perhaps a thief has stolen them."

Obi and Nelson disappeared down the dusty road.

The second part of Ike's plan had worked.

Chapter
| **14** |

After Obi and Nelson had gone Chinwe and Emeka walked into Chief Agu's compound. After all, Nelson had told them to look after the house. They had a right to be there – well, that was what they would say if anybody asked.

In fact they very much hoped that nobody would ask. They hoped that nobody would see them. They had work to do.

Chinwe and Emeka did not go to the house. Instead they walked round the corner to the garage. As Obi had seen, the doors were shut tight.

"Are they locked?" Chinwe asked.

Chinwe held her breath as Emeka turned the big metal handle. It was heavy and rusty, but it moved easily. Then Emeka pulled the doors of the garage wide open.

"Good," said Emeka. "Now the car can drive straight in."

Chinwe felt weak inside. She licked her lips. If Emeka could be brave, so could she.

The garage was empty, as they expected.

"Have you got the keys?" asked Emeka. "You can do the next bit. You're better at that sort of thing than me. I'm sometimes a bit clumsy. I'll keep watch for you."

If Chinwe had not been so frightened she would have laughed. A bit clumsy! If anybody could drop something or trip over his own feet it was Emeka.

Chinwe was carrying a strong bag, and from it she took a big bunch of keys. That morning Eyes and Ears had collected every key that they could find. Some were big, some were small, some were new, some were old and rusty. Some of the keys had just been lying round, not used any more. Some had come from the doors in their houses, others from suitcases and boxes.

Ike had tied all the keys together on a long piece of string. He did not want to lose any of them.

Emeka stood just outside the garage door. He wanted to watch the drive. Chinwe hurried to the back of the garage, to the door of the storeroom.

The big padlock was still on the door of the storeroom, and it was still locked.

"I'm starting now," Chinwe whispered.

She worked her way along the long piece of string, trying every key in the padlock. Some were the wrong size, but some went in quite easily. None fitted though. None would turn and open it.

"Hurry, hurry," Emeka whispered. "The car will be here soon."

"I am hurrying," Chinwe replied crossly. "You come and try all the keys if you think you can do it better than me."

"No, no," cried Emeka. "You carry on."

Chinwe's fingers shook more and more, as she tried the keys. It was no good. None of them fitted the padlock.

"I can't do it, Emeka. None of them are any good. None of them will turn."

"Try again," Emeka told her. "There are so many keys that one of them must work. But hurry."

"That's the problem. I'm hurrying too much. I've got to take my time."

"All right, take your time then. But just get on and do it. If Ike gave the message the car will be here soon."

Chinwe took a deep breath. She would be slow and careful this time. Emeka was right. One of the keys would open the padlock.

This time Chinwe did not try all the keys, just the ones that went into the padlock easily. And at last one of them turned. Almost before she knew what had happened, the padlock was open.

"I've done it," she called.

"Great. Now untie the key and put it in a safe place. And leave the padlock where it is."

Emeka did not have to tell Chinwe this. She already knew what to do next. In no time at all she was standing beside Emeka. The key was safely in her pocket.

"Now all we can do is wait," said Emeka. "I'll go behind this door. You go behind the other one. Let's hope that the car will be here soon."

"And let's hope that Obi keeps Nelson away from the compound," Chinwe added.

Everything suddenly seemed very quiet in Chief Agu's compound. Nelson's chickens – who had never escaped at all – were scratching happily in the dirt, but they were the only things that moved. The noise of traffic on the main road seemed far away.

"I hope Emeka can keep quiet," Chinwe thought.

They did not have to wait for long. Soon they heard a car on the drive. The driver braked and it slid to a stop in the garage.

"Hello, there?" they heard a voice call out.

There was no answer. Chinwe and Emeka hardly dared to breathe.

"Hello," the voice came again. "Anybody there?"

Still nothing happened.

"Hello. Anybody there?" The voice sounded worried now.

Chinwe and Emeka heard the car door open. Feet moved across the floor of the garage. What would the driver do next?

"I don't like this. I'm not waiting here much longer for any customer. It's too dangerous."

The driver was talking to himself. Would he leave? Would he wait in the car? Would he stay in the garage?

The feet came to the garage door and stopped. They were only centimetres away from Emeka and Chinwe.

Then the feet moved to the back of the garage. The padlock banged against the storeroom door as it squeaked open.

"NOW!" screamed Emeka, and rushed into the garage. Chinwe was right behind him. Nothing could stop them now.

The storeroom door crashed shut. The key turned in the padlock.

The third part of Ike's plan had worked.

Chapter

| **15** |

"What . . .? What . . .?"

Emeka and Chinwe leaned back against the door of the storeroom. Kicks and blows rained down on the other side but they took no notice.

"Let me out! Let me out! Just wait until I get my hands on you. I'll kill you."

"Got him," Emeka laughed. "That'll show the fat man. Let him see what it's like to be locked up."

The shouts from the other side of the storeroom door got louder and louder. The fat man did not really understand what had happened.

"What's going on? What do you want? Is it money you want? I'll pay you, just let me out."

The kicks on the storeroom door got harder and harder. The padlock shook, but the door was strong.

"Will he escape, Emeka?" Chinwe asked. "Can he get out? Will he beat the door down, do you think?"

"Never," said Emeka.

"And he won't get out through the window, like you did?" Chinwe was still worried. "He won't escape that way, will he?"

"No way," Emeka said. "He's much too fat. That's why Ike gave the message to him, not to the other smuggler."

"Are you sure?" asked Chinwe. "Really sure?"

Emeka nodded his head.

"Really sure," he said. "The window's very small, and our friend inside is very fat. He's safe in there for a while."

The noise from the storeroom was terrible. Chinwe could hardly hear Emeka. Feet were kicking the door and hands were beating it. All the time the shouting went on.

Emeka and Chinwe were so busy in the garage that they

did not see anything outside. They did not notice another big black car come up the drive and stop. They did not hear a man get out.

"What's going on here?" the man asked. "What are you doing in my garage?"

Chinwe and Emeka turned round. As they did so Ike arrived, hot, tired and dirty. He had run all the way from the market. Behind him was Obi. She did not want to miss anything either.

"What's going on here?" the man asked again, very firmly.

"It's Chief Agu!" cried Ike.

"He's come back!" shouted Emeka.

"He's not in America!" called Chinwe.

"Chief Agu's home," whispered Obi. "Oh I'm so glad."

The shouting and the kicking and the beating on the door was still going on. The man in the storeroom was very very angry.

"What's going on?" Chief Agu asked a third time. "I want to know what's happening."

Everybody tried to explain at once.

"We caught a smuggler . . ."

"He was selling cloth in the market . . ."

"He stole Mother's money . . ."

"He tied Emeka up in a sack and locked him . . ."

"One at a time!" roared Chief Agu over all the noise.

"You," he said, pointing to Ike, "you're the oldest. You tell me."

So Ike told him everything. He explained how Eyes and Ears had found out about the smugglers. He explained that they were using the chief's compound while he was away. He explained the plan to catch the smugglers.

"I gave him a message to meet a customer here," he said.

"And I got Nelson out of the way," Obi broke in. "He didn't know what was going on."

"And we locked the smuggler in the storeroom," Chinwe and Emeka added. "That's what's going on. We locked the smuggler in the storeroom. He's trying to break out."

By this time Eyes and Ears were not just talking to Chief Agu. Hundreds of people had heard the noise. A great crowd had gathered to see the fun. Men, women and children filled the compound.

"Let him out," said Chief Agu in his firm voice. "Let's see what this man has to say. If he is a smuggler he won't escape. There are too many people around."

Chinwe took the key from her pocket. She put it in the padlock and turned it slowly. The door of the storeroom opened. Out walked the fat man.

"These children are telling lies," he said. "They're bad, naughty children. Their parents should beat them."

"What are you saying?" Chief Agu asked him.

"I'm saying that I'm not a smuggler," said the fat man.

"It's not true. I'm not a smuggler. These children are telling lies. I'm just visiting this town. I drove my car in here by mistake. I thought this was my friend's house. And these children locked me in that storeroom. I'm not a smuggler."

Ike frowned. He was not going to let the fat man get away with this.

"Please, Chief Agu," he cried. "It is true. This man is a smuggler. I can prove it."

Chief Agu looked first at the fat man and then at Ike. He did not know which of them to believe.

"Prove it," he said at last to Ike. "If you're telling lies this man goes free at once. If he's a smuggler I'll make sure he's punished."

Ike frowned at the fat man.

"This is your car, you say?"

The fat man nodded his head.

"Then open the boot," Ike told him. "Open the boot."

"No, I . . . I can't . . ." the fat man tried to say. "I . . . I haven't got . . . I won't . . ."

"Open the boot," roared Chief Agu.

"I'll do it," Ike cried. "I'll prove this man's a smuggler."

As Ike opened the boot there was a shout from the crowd. Everybody pushed forward to see what was happening.

The boot was full of smuggled cloth. It lay there in great rolls, lace in every colour of the rainbow. It was the most beautiful cloth that the people had ever seen.

"Take him into my house," said Chief Agu. "He won't escape. Send for the police."

"No, let me go," the fat man begged. "I'll tell you everything. I'll give you the names of my friends. I'll tell you where they're staying. Just let me go and I'll help you."

"You'll tell the police everything," said Chief Agu. "And then you'll be punished."

He turned to Eyes and Ears.

"Well done," he said. "You can be proud of yourselves."

Ike was already taking his notebook out of his pocket.

"Thank you, Chief Agu," he said. "Can we go home now? I've got something important to do."

Already available in **Mactracks**

Starters

The Hunter's Dream   Meja Mwangi
Martha's Mistakes   Lorna Evans
Fiki Learns to Like Other People   Lauretta Ngcobo
Zulu Spear   Olive Langa
Mercy in a Hurry   Mary Harrison
Tanzai and Bube   John Haynes
Karabo's Accident   Frances Cross
The Little Apprentice Tailor   Marcus Kamara
Follow that Footprint!   Jill Inyundo
We're Still Moving!   Damian Morgan

Sprinters

Mystery of the Sagrenti Treasure   Ekow Yarney
Eyes and Ears   Brenda Ferry
Eyes and Ears Work Hard   Brenda Ferry
One in a Million   Emma Johnson
Map on the Wall   Colin Swatridge
Magic Trees   Jenny Vincent
Dark Blue is for Dreams   Rosina Umelo
Find out from Fossils   Lorna Evans *(non-fiction)*

Runners

Guitar Wizard   Walije Gondwe
Star   Nandi Dlovu
Days of Silence   Rosina Umelo
Never Leave Me   Hope Dube
Juwon's Battle   Victor Thorpe
Fineboy   Maurice Sotabinda

Winners

Halima   Meshack Asare
Foli Fights the Forgers   Kofi Quaye
Jojo in New York   Kofi Quaye
Presents from Mr Bakare   Mary Harrison
Sara's Friends   Rosina Umelo
Trouble in the City   Hope Dube
Let the Sunbird Sing   James Ngumy
Kayo's House   Barbara Kimenye
Be Beautiful   Lydia Eagle and Barbara Jackson *(non-fiction)*
Sport in Africa   Ossie Stuart *(non-fiction)*